Just Another Sunrise

Poems to the Sun

by

Fred Simpson

What people are saying about Just Another Sunrise

Sunrise & sunrise & sunrise. Simple beauty in infinite diversity. Like the sunrises shared in Fred Simpson's *Just Another Sunrise*, these poems are deceptively simple, revealing more depth as you sit with them, as you take in each new dawn while it develops. This quiet hymn of a book in red and gold is a welcome addition to your bookshelf; each poem is a new morning.

– Matthew Hupert, Author, Ism is a Retrovirus

Poet Fred Simpson displays his painterly eye, lyricism, philosophical bent, penchant for innovation, and essentially optimistic life verve in *Just Another Sunrise*, a full-length volume of verse that will leave the sensitive reader a wiser and better person. Mr. Simpson shows his capacity to allow thematic depth and uniqueness of technique to come together in a most felicitous union in this impressive and satisfying bardic debut. Dive in, and you will never perceive an East River sunrise in quite the same way.

– Barbara Hantman, Corresponding Secretary, Fresh Meadows Poets

Fred Simpson is a prolific poet. His poems are heartfelt and engaging. I am happy that he has chosen to share his poems with the world.

– Joan Reese, Artist, Poet, Blogger

Who else watches the exact time of the sunrise or the sunset. Whitman called him astronomer; who else watches time but the gaze of Banneker; the Sufi or Rumi with all the mystique and mystery, with all the ascension and grandiosity. When you read [Fred Simpson's] words, not only will you levitate but you will rise and be possessed.

– Robert Gibbons, Author, Close to the Tree

Exceeding all other creative expression, poetry is the most organic; a seed that starts with sophomoric sentimentality and later grows into a tree overlooking a forest of human experiences. As a poet, Fred Simpson is such a tree that has experienced every season. Above all his experiences, the sun has illuminated his growth. From birth to maturity, the sidereal cycles are there in his work. "Beneath his branches I was pleased to read his leaves."

– *Bob McNeil, Artist and Writer*

An inherent source of wonder might be within oneself's consciousness of poetry; it might be that nowhere is oneself's uniqueness more evident than in such consciousness as that of Fred Simpson.

– *Harry Ellison, Poet and Poetry Teacher*

First the concept: a series of poems to the sun rising across the East River above the rooftops of Queens and Brooklyn. Not just imagistic odes, but full-blooded poems that explore a man's relation to the living being of the rising sun. Then the execution: the relation of poet to sunrise is as rich, real, dissonant, and unpredictable as any relation of human to human. Each poem tackles a different sunrise, sings its own song in its own voice, bares its own emotional heart and soul, is painted in its own imagery. The images are instantaneous in their evocation. The voices range from prayerful to playful, serious to whimsical, angry to conciliatory, muscular to elegant, bitchy to tender, sassy to rhapsodic. Some poems will remind you of Crane's classical homage to the Brooklyn Bridge. And then there are voices and styles that come straight off the street of the city that runs in Fred's blood: rap, blues, reggae, jazz, hip-hop, other musical forms that put in appearances and play surprising solos in these poems. And that is what I find most striking about them. Their vibrant musical versatility. How mood and voice and tone and attitude can skip and turn on an eighth note. How Fred's talent as a musician and songwriter infuses each poem with music and each sunrise with the life and lyricism of a song. A brilliant, honest, provocative, and original collection.

– *Max Zimmer, Author,* If Where You're Going Isn't Home

Just Another Sunrise

Poems to the Sun

Copyright © 2014 by Fred Simpson
All rights reserved

ISBN 978-0-9903670-0-0

Cover concept by Elesia Simpson

Cover photograph by Fred Simpson

Cover design and execution by Max Zimmer

Interior design by Max and Toni Zimmer of The Writers Group

Sunrise poem xii, "No Sunrise Today," previously appeared in *The Venetian Hour, Dinner with the Muse Vol. II* anthology, Evie Ivy, Editor

We are all,

every one of us,

under the sun.

For my father,

Fred Simpson Sr.

Contents

i	Dawn Prayer	3
ii	Speed of Light	5
3.13.12	Just Another Sunrise, East River, New York City	9
	Pasodoblé, Me and You	11
4.8.12	Looks Like a No-Show	13
5.16.12	Keep Dreamin'	15
4.9.12	Anticlimactic	17
4.10.12	Morning Rush	19
4.25.12	Estimated Wait Time for My Call To Be Answered...	21
5.3.12	Problem: Great Expectation	23
5.23.12	Solution: Fly Away	25
5.17.12	Staying Power	27
5.19.12	Merrily Earth Rolls Along	29
5.24.12	No Sunrise Today	31
5.28.12	Time Travel	33
6.7.12	Levantine Lines-of-Sight	35
6.15.12	Come Out Swinging	37
6.25.12	Peek-a-Boo	39
7.01.12	Master Stroke	41
	Undercover Reveille	43
8.19.12	Eureka! For Sunday-Morning-Forecast-Delight	45
8.29.12	*Solace*	47
10.6.12	HappyHappyHappy Decamper	51
10.11.12	Fiction Science	53
10.26.12	Best-Laid Plans	57
3.24.13	Full Circle	59
	Post Mortem	61
	Fun Sun Stuff	63
	Notes	65
	Acknowledgements	67
	About the Poet	69

Dawn Prayer

The sun is my shepherd.
I shall not want.
Earth beneath my feet
turns toward the light,
then away into darkness.

I sleep in rhythm
with East River waves,
be they calm or disturbed.
At dawn I wake in hope
of your coming brightness.

Speed of Light

Sweeping changes to the sky
are swiftest not in dark of night
nor mid-day when the sun is high;
not in twilight though its vistas mesmerize.

My chameleon sky can morph
from airy blue to misty grey.
Fluid reds, golds, tangerines, pinks –
like silk scarves – touch and swirl.
Whole panoramas shift:
magic tricks unexplained.

Bold mid-day/lush twilight/stoic night
no match
for fleet eye-opening skies
of dawn.

Sunrise Poems

i – xxiv

Time Frame

Random early mornings, March to October 2012
Dawn Revisited March 24, 2013

i. sunrise 3/13/2012

Just Another Sunrise / East River / New York City

Again
against soft-blue sky
not far above horizon –
streaks of orange tinged with grey....

My eyes anticipate things to come;
namely, the sun.
I try to pick the spot you'll first appear;
you give no hint.
No segment of horizon starts to brighten.
Tenuous daylight all you offer.
Reveal yourself! I wait for you to rise.

O,
beyond all remembrance of dawns,
beyond all imaginable brightness,
how many watts infuse my soul!
What shore due east,
what Brooklyn, Queens,
what floor beneath my feet?!
Only you exist.
Smooth like a curtain-rise
on this opening scene,
white-hot disc ascending
fills my window;
enlivens me.
This moment:
all there is.

Ablaze with liquid amber,
soon you will be full round, blinding.
Yet, I continue to stare;
until by sleight-of-hand you lay
a gossamer swath of silver on the river,
tempting me to walk upon its surface like a god.

Got to go outside; bask in your new light.
My eyes, never jaded at the sight of you.
Nothing can match Earth's rotation
giving birth to morning.

Helios, your magnitude revealed.

ii. sunrise

*Pasodoblé,** Me and You

I yearn to wake wide-eyed in broad bare desert.
Risk my cameras, left and right,
to ogle you straight on, Saharan sun.

Waterside I search for you
through dark strips of grey.
Reddish pink peeks out.
Sneaky Helios, already rising.
S l o w l y your top appears;
then *swiftly-all-the-rest,*
above a banked-down density of clouds.
No visible circumference,
just a blur of white energy
dominates the eastern sky.
Look away hot minute to save my eyes,
you morph into a perfect disc;
concentrated, radiating.
Try to get my mind around
seeing you whole; floating, lording.
Seem slightly flattened at the poles.

Your stroke in tangerine
runs strong and thin
from Newtown Creek
to dissipate while widening
toward Manhattan shore.
Sparklers glistening,
reflected on this tidal strait
your light a subtle threat
to my captured vision.
Time stops
whenever you hold my gaze.

Put pen to paper, transcribe this rapture.
Flashes blot out parts of what I write.
Scribble on with faith
each word will be deciphered
when pupils are restored to normal sight.

Dare not stare directly at your climb.
Preserve my vision for thousands more ascensions –
future dawns and all the times I will summon
vivid risings etched indelibly.

What else can up my spirits and as frequently?
Perhaps to watch you set in western sky.
Unfurl a hot pink canvas
stroked with emerald and violet;
wispy clouds contrasting those tightly wound
like aircraft vapor trails.

Might be worth a stroll across town
to catch your twilight
of satin cloth,
edgy chalk pastels.

Pasodoblé: (Spanish) double step; a dance for two in march time. Also associated with bullfighting.

iii. sunrise 4/8/2012

Looks Like a No-Show

*Three hundred-thirty thousand times Earth's volume/
big ball of hydrogen/
nine thousand-plus surface degrees Fahrenheit/
pushing out helium –
did you have a good rest last night?
This morning you are shy.*

6:15 a.m. Woke up late
to a wide orange stripe below ominous grey.
Rushed outside; sun was having second thoughts
about coming out to play.

Despite your apprehension to appear,
my expectation does not fade.
I'll bet you rise right around... *there*,
where grey is all but erased.

6:40 a.m. Looks like you're setting!
"Overcast" is the word.
Breeze hints of probable rain.
I begin to doubt your skyward campaign.

Dedicated jogger appears;
a boxer-in-training.
As if to keep the rain at bay,
he jab-jab-jabs at the air.

But you are movie star,
muted behind limo's tinted glass.
Riding low in the backseat,
star presence felt nonetheless.

Slice of blue reveals itself
through sky now darker grey.
Mixed signals? No.
For me, nothing more than a slight delay.

*Helios, please disburse the darkness
of impending rain.*

7:20 a.m., sky lightens.
Odds now favor that you *will* show.
If not in all your glory,
then steady like a stone....

Ascend triumphant through dense clouds
that hardly soften your glow.
But faint mother-of-pearl is all that emanates.
Your healing rays a distant dream I've known.

Ever hopeful I pray
for one sun shower
to generate a rainbow
followed by your heat.

So much for denial.
Promising signs nowhere to be seen.
Odds are you will not show today;
so, *"Hasta la vista."*

Easter Sunday, April eighth,
I'm givin' up the wait.
Leavin' you in that lurch of clouds,
I am goin' off to church.

iv. sunrise 5/16/2012

Keep Dreamin'

An artist with lightest touch
works in powders, the residue of chalk.
Flats of fingertips rub a wide strip –
honey dijon in hue –
not quite parallel to the horizon.

In dingy cotton clouds,
one small fissure reveals
proof of your masked presence.
I wait for you, coy star,
and drift into a dream:
Earth's belt, Gulf of Guinea,
zero lat, zero longitude...
from deck of ocean liner I see
equatorial sunrise, l a r g e; no – h u g e,
eclipse all East River memories of you.

Forget ocean liner, any old floating bucket will do.
To be on that sea, nothing in between me and sunrise
the moment you signal dawn!

Burn away the haze.
I long to see you face to face.
How many more overcast mornings
can I wake up in a funk
to write about the *invisible* sun?

Give me a blood-orange dawn;
your rays wide on the river
making waters dance,
my spirit step lively.

Great! Didn't have to wait.
Your heart pulses heat and piercing light.
Must stare.
Cumulus, please protect my eyes.

Meet the fool who gets his wish –
sun bum-rushed by clouds.
Gilded bedroom walls suddenly awash
in sullen grey.

Enough of your ambivalence.
Close the blinds.
Switch on the gooseneck;
bulb soft white
like the moon sometimes.
Helios, maybe I'll catch you
on your downward slide.

This dark morning
might as well be night.

v. sunrise 4/9/2012

Anticlimactic

Call it luck. I wake up
to fledgling daylight.
Get dressed; go outside.
Want no pane between us when you rise.

Surprise! Moon still out;
bright over my right shoulder.
Chilly this morning; muscular breeze.
Long Island City skyline silhouetted clean.

Two cloud wisps materialize:
one reindeer leaping
alongside some Rorschach shape.
Each soon vanquished by the wind.

Is this Spring?
I'm shivering!
Two pigeons walk,
beak-to-tail in tandem.

They fly off. To bed? Where I should be!
Six-o-five I came out;
six-thirty a.m. now,
I'm trying not to freeze.

Patience... you're worth the wait...
kudos if you reach a forecasted high
of sixty-five Fahrenheit... oh yeah, the moon...
up higher... fading... fading... Luna, goodbye....

At last, in a stretch of steeples, floating billboards,
rooftop water tanks – a sign: soft orange on horizon
like a distant conflagration.
Now I know exactly where you'll rise.

How quickly you ignite.
Best I can do – a peripheral glance.
Your image blots my longhand
as I document your climb.

Sun circle superimposed
wherever I stare
rides on a breeze
that only pretends to die.

Cold hands, yes, but why
do I feel cold inside?
Sight of you
has always warmed me up.

I concede to this chill wind
despite your blitz of light.
Helios, don't take offense.
I'm off to buy potato chips.

Yes,
potato chips
at seven a.m.
I need the salt.

vi. sunrise 4/10/2012

Morning Rush

Made it outside just in time.
Horizon more pink than orange.
No trace of morning moon.
River breeze kind.
Anticipation primed.
Imagination going into overdrive:
Suppose one day, there was no sun.
Well then there'd be no 'us'.

Gulls in flight, airplane gains height;
barge marked 'Bouchard' slowly glides –
props, minor players, set the stage.

Up, bring up the footlights;
up from the horizon!
Your rays tinge rough cotton clouds.
One column of light positively inspirational,
points straight up.

Oops, there you are!
Seem small today; no less mesmerizing.
Gull lands smooth on the river
like a base runner sliding into first;
his or her head same angle as mine,
watching you rise.
Already you've cleared Greenpoint's horizon.
Birds provide a soundtrack for the scene
as my eyes play tricks on me....

I see not one, but three silhouetted suns,
arced, ascending into clouds
like a time lapse photograph.
Fact: there's only one of you.
Distance: ninety-three million miles;
close enough to ogle,
like I would some hot *femme fatale*.

Strange.
Never thought of you in female terms.
Just masculine, like the deity you are
to those who wax their boards
and those who in their hearts
need to follow the sun.

I'll harness a jot of your energy,
just enough to get me off this bench.
A pinch of inspiration
from the way you light the day/
lead it fearless into night,
will put me in a state of mind
my only limit is your sky.

Helios, it is my turn to rise.

vii. sunrise 4/25/2012

Estimated Wait Time for My Call to be Answered...

Daylight happens sooner than sunrise.
River calm.
No threat of rain.
Thought forty degrees Fahrenheit would feel chillier.
Dressed for it – sweater under light leather.
This morning checked your e.t.a.:
six-o-two a.m. *Can't wait!*
Guess I'm having a love affair with the sun.

Five fifty eight a.m.
Solitude shattered
by a man with cigarette, thermos, cell phone.
I have a cell too but I'm not yapping.
He finally shuts up; I breathe a sigh.
Clouds take on an orange tinge.
My "friend" with cell phone, thermos, cigarette,
turns on his heel.
Say to myself, *thank you; goodbye!*
Is he even aware
a spectacular show is about to begin?
Does he even care?
Anyway, good riddance.
Is that unkind?

Now the *doorman* is outside, not fifty feet away,
having a smoke.
Typical Manhattan: four a.m., six a.m., *anytime a.m.*,
desert island, no/crowded, hurried place, yes.
Night owls will attest
it's normal not to be the only soul on the street,
wee hours of a New York weeknight.

All-nite supermarts, crowded aisles two a.m.
Traffic jams three a.m. –
testimony to a city's vibrancy –
but I often crave peace, s p a c e . . .
like now.
I can do without the doorman taking his break.

Come, sun.
Put me under your gold-spun spell.
Six-o-eight but you're not late.
I'm sure you were up at six-o-two,
easternmost Montauk Point.
Takes time for Earth to rotate hundred-twenty miles
to bring you into my Manhattan view.

Wild excuses
in hopes you'll shine directly;
as if you even know on the surface
or deep within your core
that you alone sustain me.

There you are... big today.
Glaring.
Can't make out your shape
through that wild *avant garde* burning halo.

Does appearance matter? Yes.
It matters you appeared!
I like to think you heard my plea.
String of grey lifeless dawns is cut.
This morning I'm ecstatic you fill my eyes.
So glad you decided to show up.

viii. sunrise 5/3/2012

Problem: Great Expectation

In bed open my eyes.
Six a.m. not too late to see you rise.
Get up, pee; head to double windows.
Raise the blinds.

That's what it's all about, isn't it?
Raising the blinds
so we can truly see.

Six-o-five, overcast sky;
no rain on my windows way up high.
Go outside into fine spray –
lasts but a second.
Not enough to make me damp;
enough to rain on my expectation.

Minutes later muted light seeps,
bleeds, through blotchy sky;
proof you have already risen.
Disappointment is understatement!
You rose hidden behind the clouds,
out of my line of sight.

These days my soul is tired.
Dreams teeter in peril
of falling off the realm of possibility.
Veil of middle age stretches
for ninety-three million miles.
The hope: my vision never clouds, never fades.

These days, this firmament infirm
with shifting puffs and powders
blocks you out, keeps you at bay.
Triggers my version of an adage:
Your absence makes my heart grow fonder;
more desperate for your rays.

Maybe later on you'll grace me with your brilliance,
Ball-of-Fire, Mighty One, Ra, Inti, Kinich Ahau,
Sol, my sun –
Where *are* you?
Where
have you gone?

ix sunrise 5/23/2012

Solution: Fly Away

*Clear days, rainy days, thunder, lightning,
occasional sun shower –
its bonus rainbow not enough...
anything and everything can play
on a New York spring day,
fickle month of May.*

Five fifty-four a.m.
Helios, will you shine;
turn this grey dawn to blue?
There *is* hope as sky lightens.
Silhouettes of buildings take on depth
through the murk.
Is that an orange glow? No –
a figment of my desire to see you rise;
to catch a glimpse of you.

Fewer lights across the river.
Some doused by new-falling rain?
Rain. All the more likely now
you won't show today.

I think 'shooting star'
when a string of street lamps dies,
programmed by computer to expire.
Morning rushes on at breakneck speed;
panics me. Do not want to spend
another day without your heat.

One brave gull flaps by
through thin broth of rain.
This bird, agent of truth that *I* must fly
to feel consistent warmth.
My head is *so* not here
on this dim Manhattan shore.
No rays today transfix my eyes.
No you to hold my gaze.

By noon will you have broken through?
I think not.
The thing for me to do is hop a plane...

Let tropic heat envelope me
where sweet aromas bring
heady fruit of Caribbean dreams.
Better odds you'll be there when I wake
to glide through limpid waters;
your rays refracting hints of blue-green sea
in crests of docile waves.
I'll drift away...
fly away....

x. sunrise 5/17/2012

Staying Power

Eyes closed,
lids are photographic plates
playing back a stark fragment of you
exposed through the clouds....
Your rays, soft music heard off-stage,
take shape; crescendo to just shy of red.
Your rays, harbingers of you,
burst through cotton....

Gather strength; set fire to horizon.
Tips of flames tinged bluish green
dart/dance like serpents' tongues.
I gaze to confirm
this animated conflagration
is no mirage.

One-two-three you're high above
a low-slung bank of clouds;
headed west to pass the torch.
Electric New York night awaits.

Day out/day out you set
beyond the Palisades;
burn and never rest.
Thanks to you, tomorrow
will be another day.

xi. sunrise 5/19/2012

Merrily Earth Rolls Along

At five twenty-two a.m. simple things continue to amaze,
like daylight happening well before the sun appears.
Dimmer-switch swiftly ramped up in eastern sky.
Light intensifies, accompanied by strains of harp strings.

You rise in the east;
but east is slightly farther left
of where you rose in *early* spring.
Time passes, sunrise shifts.
Nothing stays the same.
As a child I thought
until an embarrassing age,
that there *was* a Santa Claus.

Pencil or charcoal might be
Leonardo da Vinci's twenty-first century choice
to sketch a backlit Long Island City skyline.
Cluster of buildings under construction,
cranes askew like giant antennae gone wild
atop skeletal steel frames – modern sculpture.
Dark foil to pink horizon light.

Upward, pink meets powdery blue.
Stage is set for a magic trick:
a ball intensely luminous, huge,
will suspend itself in mid-air.

"Ladies and gentlemen, ascending now for your viewing
pleasure, my star! Nothing brighter in this world, more
warming, searing, than its light."

Another day, another holler.
To Helios, a 'shout-out', as they say.
Barring catastrophic Earth-ending events
I wonder what they'll say a hundred years from now?
What will they call it
when someone gives a shout-out to the sun?

xii. sunrise 5/24/2012

No Sunrise Today

Across the river,
strings of street lamps not-quite-white,
and rows of pale green factory lights
trail off into dawn.
Bright spots, these horizontal streams of tears,
shine through a soup of grey emotion.
Rain on my double window re-affirms:
this density will stay
to impede your rays for hours.

On a cloudless, rainless day
you would be rising, white-hot.
Blinding, daring me to stare.
Up-up above the landscape –
swift, you would be whole by now ....

Your entrances are finely etched.
I select from them on rainy days like this.
Vivid, how you played with my eyes;
held them to relentless light,
punished them for gazing.
Dark shapes, light; light shapes, dark;
like negatives of photographs.

Silhouette-to-solid/solid-to-silhouette,
your solar image repeated
until you released it from my tired lids;
to remain forever lucid in the mind.

xiii. sunrise 5/28/2012

Time Travel

5:37 a.m.
Clouds spread out,
eastern sky.
Molecules speeding,
heated by your nearness.
Swiftly you appear,
concise blinding disc.
A constant for all things bright.

6:07 a.m.
Circumference no longer distinct.
Radiant, you flaunt yourself.
River waves liven to a quick step
under your gaze.
Coast Guard Cutter complicates the dance
with its widening-triangle wake.
Risen higher you are discernibly round;
halo evident now.

On your trajectory:
you will dust Manhattan canyon walls with shadow.
Sidewalks will swelter, affirming your heat.
As in the past, blight my vision of the page
when I try to write down the ways you amaze.
Yours the knack to simultaneously blind and clarify.

6:28 a.m.
Clouds are your platform.
I bask in you, Helios, on days like today –
flip sides of winter downers, those frigid days
that seep negativity/sap energy/I struggle in a trough/
too often concede to the grey/
shoulders hunched into concavities of spirit.

Today I stand straight;
stare directly into your golden face.
Sustained.

Ever get tired?
Have days when you are not ready to rise
but you do it anyway?
I have to track you sometime;
look for any signs of fatigue
when you're about to set
at the end of a long daylight-savings day....

I'll make a note of it: *Twilight, West Side, one day soon, GO to watch the sun set.*

xiv. sunrise 6/7/2012

Levantine Lines-of-Sight

*I have witnessed none of Christ's miracles –
changing water into wine, Resurrection, Ascension –
nor am I a prophet blessed by revelation.
Yet, I do believe.*

Today I saw a golden orb
rise up and pierce the clouds.
Forgive me, Lord, sun worshippers are
completely comprehended now.
I feel them in my core.

More than a patina inspiring faith,
Sol, your onslaught opens me up.
Regrettably I avert my eyes
to protect against your rays.

Airy puffs of cotton appear.
Welcome, they soften your shine
while I imagine a freedom in blindness –
no colors, no physical lines.

No inverted images, eye-to-brain.
With other stimuli –
touch, smell, sound, taste –
the mind is free to form impressions.

Blind or with sight,
insanity potential bane
of an over-active imagination;
tendency to get carried away
with all-too-vivid visualization.

Time for me to blast off from the sun!
Come down easy. Take an Earthly stroll –
in the heat of any desert will do;
the Negev, for one.

Love the sound of that name, "Negev."
Immediately Sol envelopes me.
Heat waves move the terebinth trees.
I am rapt.

xv. sunrise 6/15/2012

Come Out Swinging

I am mortal, awaiting the godly sun.
Anticipation not peripheral,
it is the main event.

5:31 a.m.
Don't want to talk about billowy clouds
the color of cigarette smoke.
I'll occupy my mind with other observations –
stress-relief while hoping you will show.

Seagull heads downriver and back for morning exercise.
I must do something physical: start jogging,
play some basketball (try not to fracture anything).
Goal is to *extend* my lifespan and longevity has a price.
Got to get my head into the game.

Did I just say that?
Sports metaphors be damned!
But these clouds *are* the sky's defensive line,
preventing you from breaking through.
Ooh, the game-changer:
an opening in all that grey glows molten gold.
No doubt I'll see your brazen helmet soon.

6:10 a.m.
Ceiling lifts, only to concede
a stubborn off-white sky.
Still no you.
Mid-June, this far into morning,
you *must* be up already; just not visible
behind a woeful lack of blue.

Three pigeons, one starling come near.
No crumbs to throw, I walk away;
decide to break some bread –
bacon, eggs, grits – transference
for what my eyes have not been fed.

If I liked Bloody Marys I'd have one or two;
figure what to do with this early-morning energy.
Energy, the word reminds me of you
who stood me up; a fool-in-waiting.

Am I disappointed? Let me count the ways.
No. *Keep my spirits up! Let the games begin!*
Perhaps with a sporting phrase or two...

It's the opening tip / I'm in the starting gate /
Ready for that first pitch – high and outside –
I resist / "Ball One!"
Through stubborn clouds you signal once more
for me to come out swinging / "Round Two" /
I answer your muted bell.

xvi. sunrise 6/25/2012

Peek-a-Boo

Charcoal grey clouds shaped like mountains
float dark against thick atmosphere.
Sky closes ranks.
Peeking out, you bleed orange
through one last slit.
Otherwise I would have missed you –
been left wondering, 'Are you up yet?'

What I wouldn't do for a sunny day!

What I *would* do
is banish all clouds,
level Long Island City's skyline –
coal-dust-ugly in this dawn's light –
for an unobstructed view of the horizon.
Then ogle your smooth ascent
as witness to the start of a pristine day.

Born into a different ethos
I would offer human sacrifice;
beseech you to smile on us, shine.
Your breath, the warmth that enfolds;
you whom crops, fruit-bearing trees,
turn to face.
These days I just pray for sun;
try not to be depressed by too much grey,
too much rain.

*Six fifty-five a.m. Brief was your rising... quickly
you were cloaked... so much day yet to come...
already you are gone.*

xvii. sunrise 7/1/2012

Master Stroke

Unlike days I stared,
captured by your spun gold,
eyes in peril,
today I am in control.
Can look away.
Don't know why I am free
to peer across the river;
survey at leisure
the coast of Brooklyn/Queens.

Buildings, trees, are charcoal shadows –
color of night just before you arrive
to joust with overcast skies,
lay low behind proscenium of clouds;
loose a spray that gently wakes,
or with great fanfare, rouses the day.

What effects does your westward-moving
palette hold for steeples, car-filled streets,
buildings with glass faces,
East and Hudson Rivers' flow?
How will they wear your changing coat?

An artist can only try
to duplicate your light
as it moves over surfaces.
Oils, pastels, watercolors held
to one still-life moment
once paint sets and dries.

Big motion now!
Swiftly up,
above the skyline,
surface gases unsuppressed,
you wear a wild hellion hairstyle.

Heat comes to mind,
the kind that leads to economy of motion;
mercifully slows my relentless quick-city life.
Enables me to learn from the pace of tropics
the origin, essence of things.

Fertile Crescent Garden was not of snow.
Helios, you burn away the haze
from sky, mind, soul.

xviii. sunrise

Undercover Reveille

Awake in bed me and my legal pad no desire
to be mobile or vertical through the blinds
I see grey no danger to my eyes from glare
nor to my spirit though I am cool Helios
to your lack of morning luster one reason
I'm not a good conversationalist my mind
makes cryptic connections prompted by dismal
sky I ponder your rays maybe it's true absence
makes the heart grow fonder *then...*
you invade my chamber your rays make me
squint infringe on the comfort of my bed heat up
my sheets which I have to throw off you
beckon me to rise with the shine of a room
now tinged with gold leaf I must raise blinds
open flood gates to your energy your rays
unseen but for the medium through which
they travel unseen but for what they illuminate
sometimes sketching rainbows on the way.
Life in this hemisphere is under your stare each
surface in this room bathed wallet coins atop my
chest of drawers sweater I didn't hang up last night
warts and wonders of the world outside garbage barge
on the river gulls lighter-than-air in flight
pedestrians look like human ants twenty-two floors
below my window screeching brakes honking horns
I just get the visual from up here.
Can your light fathom pedestrian dreams traffic's
destinations no matter you manage to flatter
the soul-less sidewalk the tarmac in tandem you
make it all look good just by shining your light Helios
you ham let me count the ways you steal the scene.

xix. sunrise 8/19/2012

Eureka! For Sunday-Morning-Forecast-Delight

*In a half-sleep nightmare I see
aggressor-planet Earth
boldly go where it has never gone:
out of orbit – to invade a red-faced Mars.
Next step: colonize.
WAIT! This just in…
Sunrise is imminent.*

Helios, this is not the first time
you have stolen the scene.
Still don't know how you pull it off –
big ball of hydrogen,
one among many suns in the cosmos.
This time you invade my dream!

Not crow of cock, but stark call of seagull
announces the hunt for his or her food
and my hunt for the vision of you.
Know exactly where to look and I will,
though sunglass-less I am unprepared
to be breathless.
Been awhile since I witnessed you rise
in a spectacle of fire.
Orange sky intensifies.
Clouds dissolve into your rays.

It is not this no-rain firmament,
soup-free ether (a pilot's dream)
nor weatherman's 'Eureka!'
for Sunday-morning-forecast-delight.
It is *you* that hold me.
You, brighter than the brightest idea;
you, gaseous solid sight.

Your halo more yellow than color of butter.
Through my window I do off-side glances
at a perfect pastry ring of light.
Diverts my sweet tooth for all forms of sugar.
Sates my craving for your eye candy.
Good thing you give off no aroma.
God save my eyes
to feed this appetite!

xx. sunrise 8/29/2012

Solace

Never have I seen horizon fire
s t r e t c h so many miles...
Ed Koch Bridge due south through Queens
to the Brooklyn side of the Williamsburg
where your light curves up
like Mona Lisa's smile.

Orange turns yellow at Newtown Creek;
a no-brainer for my hungry eyes.
I *know* this is the spot
where you will rise.

Ablaze:
bold-faced, golden, untamed beacon
shatters the horizon.
No discernible pattern,
just all over the place –
and into my head.
Close my lids,
your uninvited image remains.

Godsend:
two seagulls, India ink in motion,
lead my eyes away from danger
to a pair of diamond chips
far off in eastern sky.
One directly above the other,
each dot vertically descends; disappears.
Phenomenon I know to be
aircraft landing at JFK.

◆ 47

Sol, you've cleared the rooftops.
What history being made
will you shine on today?
Hopefully, something positive
but not too serendipity
as to trigger that niggling scale
that must balance things out;
give equal time to unpleasantness
like super storms, failing markets,
harsh realities that intrude on fairy tales
by whispering in my ear:
Sunrise is a lie.
It is Earth that moves us
into dawn, into day, into night.

No tears,
though I have rhapsodized
your grand entrances, stage east.
Imagined giant pulleys, chains,
bootstraps perhaps tanned in Hell;
each employed by dint of heat
and your sheer will
to raise you up each day in glory.

No tears
for the demise of the sunrise.
Something that never was
can never die.
Vital campfire, I am tied to your core.
You will always be my star.

Parched
when fallen snow turns black on city streets,
I long for your heat.
Quenched
when your rays inspire hyperbole of praise,
I believe every word I sing
come March, April, May, June, July, August,
September.

xxi. sunrise 10/6/2012

HappyHappyHappy Decamper

Been awhile since I tracked you;
my eyes wide, looking for signs.
Soft-glowing undersides of clouds
seem to whisper, 'You are coming.'
For this eager disciple, the question is…
"What are you waiting for?"

Guess you'll be here when you get here.
After all, it *is* autumn – days are shorter/
you rise later/exit into twilight sooner/
take your day-glow picnic with you/
then comes the dark.

Whoa!
Love it how you snap me back into the moment.
Visible behind a sheer silk veil, you rise.
Thanks to that thin filter of atmosphere, I am happy.
Happy I can stare directly at you
until you reach your apex.
By then you will have burned away the haze.

Happy.
The word sounds silly when you say it fast,
more than once.
Happyhappyhappy.
Happy not to have to look away
out of fear of harm to my vision.
Several times I've taken that risk –
inward and outward eye gazing
into your face of unbridled energy.
For safety's sake, not today, Helios.

Today I play the human frailty card
pertaining to vulnerability of my eyes.
Before I feel the heat of unimpeded rays...
before you burn any brighter...
I say, "See ya.
Have a happy!
Goodbye."

xxii. sunrise 10/11/2012

Fiction Science

1. Aureole

There is music in the glow
of distant backlit buildings.
They appear the size of Legos;
soon blotted out by the light
of a perfect ring.

I have seen only two circular rainbows.
Each stopped me in my tracks.
Neither could hold a candle
to your full-round solar halo
radiating orange-pink; filling up the sky.

On the Brooklyn side,
a hi-rise is ablaze.
Looks like a five-alarm fire!
Every window burns your morning oil, Helios;
reflecting solar power we have yet to fully tap.

Pure energy and light –
this aureole of the sun.
I choose you for my Eighth Wonder.

Then I tell myself, "Get over it;
this is everyday stuff.
Just another sunrise."
But whom am I trying to kid?
I am your stalker.
Did not know months ago
I would become addicted
to your shine.

2. Scenario

Fascinated, no; I am obsessed with the sun.
Obsession raises questions:
why this ball, sizzling-hot;
why not something made of ice,
larger than our moon,
closer to the Earth?
A frozen cube that pulses life,
in place of our sun.
One that does not rise and set
but, parallel to equator, slides
smoothly west as if on a track.
A cube, on which all life relies;
to which all life can be traced back.

Call it Freona – Freon with an 'a,'
six facets that glow;
depending on how clear
the earthmosphere that day.

Freona's orbit runs north to south,
then back up again.
Unlike most of its icy surface,
Earth's poles are verdant
(don't get as much cubeshine).
Cold spell the norm as Freona glides
in ever-widening orbit downward
(cube-wax),
until below the equator
(cube wane).
Imagine the parallax!

Much how our sunrises, sunsets differ
when seen from Antarctica versus the tropics,
so would be vistas of Freona in orbit
when viewed from the equator
versus the poles.

Your light: ice blue, clear or blinding white.
Freona, how fresh and crisp-new
the sights for our prisms,
those things that we call eyes.

3. **Antithesis**

Our sun, a furnace.
Freona, an ice box radiating cold;
freezing a world to the hardness of diamonds.

We might be called sickles;
molecules bonded by subzero temperatures
literally holding our lives together
in a jewel-like ecosystem, angular, of crystal.

Communication telepathic, without heat;
though craniums sometimes glow
when a message is received.
Alpha-quality ESP; invisible synapse network:
lines of communication open for all.
Comprehension of ideas, appreciation of art:
instantaneous for the enlightened.
Others wear stunned expressions sculpted in ice....

Sickles like snowflakes/each with unique signature/
differences barely discernible, if at all, on the surface/
one tribe/evolutionary path flash-frozen/secure/
as long as the world remains cold.

4. Fiction Science Epilogue

There is a sanity in science;
a quest for survival
implicit in the search for answers –
the desire to master by *knowing*
the hot, cold and temperate of life.

Who said it had to be
this way of fire, Helios?
Why not a giant cube of ice?
How insane a frozen world;
each flake and floe and glacier a revelation
toward fulfillment of something... perfect?

What life form, then, would we face in the mirror?
How insane is the concept of a perfect world?
No more insane
than the arbitrary design of fingers and toes
and cancers that grow.
How insane.

xxiii. sunrise 10/26/2012

Best-Laid Plans

Not easy to chronicle sunless dawns.
But suspense maintains
a fresh and watchful eye
when you are nowhere in my frame –
just pixie dust, a mist... barely luminous.
Crumbs from your high table.

Didn't set my clock.
Had to pee; that woke me up.
Seven-twelve a.m., time is right.
Can still catch your morning overture.

Soft red horizon light meets overcast grey.
Together they create an aura –
calls to mind a Jimi Hendrix tune:
Purple Haze.

Time it takes to straighten sheets
your light takes shape – a laser beam.
Through a slit in dark cloud cover,
comes one blood orange stream.

Familiar scene reprised:
forced like some young understudy,
you peek out from behind a curtain,
waiting like I wait for you to please.
Aware you're already up,
I scan the sky for further signs
in clouds that look opaque
but are in fact impassable to light.

Appear, disappear, you're such a tease.
My money says grey clouds win out,
like so many times before.
Sol, I just cannot play this game anymore.

I'm in a battle, steeling myself for winter doldrums;
milking the fleeting autumnal clock.
Blues has been known to extend its fist
and prematurely knock.

Well, whadda ya know: too little too late.
Tepid blue airbrushed here and there
with your gold; by no means radiant.
For once you are resistible.

No danger to my eyes, like when I'd stare
until, at last, break your spell; turn away.
Minutes would pass; your image still echoed.
All I could do was wait for it to fade.
This time no trumpet fanfare blares your fire.

But no hard feelings/no clock to punch/no regrets.
Goodbye, Sol, I'm lowering the blinds
and going back to bed.

xxiv. sunrise 3/24/2013

Full Circle

Earth spins nonstop.
Time flies off into the sun.
Stood right here with pen, legal pad;
three hundred sixty-five days gone-in-a-flash.

Check my outer ring
for sun spots, age spots, wrinkles,
telltale signs of damage
from our one-year fling.

You're a funny fried yolk right now,
bleeding into surrounding albumen sky.
Swift rise, you become a solid circle.
Perfect.

No color can describe
your electric brightness.
I have to squint.
You obliterate horizon line.

Been on this trip before.
I know you're about to intensify.
Won't be the first time
I am humbled by your light.

I'll just breeeathe...
        breeeathe....

Soon you will be way up,
over my right shoulder.
I will not turn my head
to worship you any longer.

Bold, I turn away from you.
One sudden thought stripped me of all tact;
prompted the need to put distance between us,
take control before the fact –

*the thought that I will lose you
on the day I die.*

Tonight a soothing luminance will enter –
neglected moon – no peril to my eyes;
at most an outside chance of drowning,
wooed by Luna's changing tides.

Sol, have a nice life.
I've been on this trip before.
Can tell you're about to intensify.
Wouldn't be the first time
I was humbled by your light.

*I'll just breeeathe...
          breeeathe....*

Post Mortem

No stress. No fear. In death there is light;
unrefracted by complicated human stuff:
flesh, family, aging, much spilt milk,
the anger of love....

Bury me face down
to cross over without sorrow,
without angst.
My last sunrise forever eclipsed,
if in the dark I did not savor it;
had no clue it was my last.

Bury me face down.
In death I'll be no less naïve.
Make it hard to ask some god,
"Did I miss the sunrise?
Which way is east?"

Face down, please,
so I cannot see the dawn.
I will not search morbid skies
for a sunrise that will never come.

Bury me face down
to wait in Earth's loam embrace.
Not for the sun.
For euphoria.

Fun Sun Stuff*

No 'x-number-of-football-fields-end-to-end' analogies here. The sun is too big for that.

Origin

Look at the sun and you are seeing an orb 4 ½ billion years young.

A supernova ended its death throes sending superheated silicon, iron & strands of other elements into a neighboring cloud of gas, collapsing it. A mixture of gas and dust gravitated to the cloud's center causing *a nuclear reaction* which *gave birth to our sun.*

Size

Let's all feel small.

Sun's diameter is about *1,392,000 km. (864, 948 mi)*, compared to Earth's 7,935 mi. Its *mass* is *2 x 10^{30} kg, 330,000 times Earth's*, and accounts for *99.86% of our Solar System.*

Content

A lot of hot air.

The *sun* is *hot plasma* interwoven with *magnetic fields*, the *cause of sun spots*. Chemically, the *sun* is *73.46% hydrogen, 24.88% helium*, and *1.69% heavier elements*, some being *oxygen, carbon, neon, iron.*

Light

Look up, feel alive. Some distant stars have already died.

Light travels from the sun to Earth in around 8 minutes, 19 seconds. Called a yellow dwarf star because its visible radiation is most intense in the yellow-green portion of the spectrum, its color is actually white.

Energy

So much the eye can and cannot see.

Sun's core generates energy at the rate of 620 million metric tons per second. A continually expanding corona creates the solar wind. Earth's magnetic field deflects it down to the poles; protecting our atmosphere. The energy this takes generates the Northern Lights.

*Sources: Wikipedia.org/wiki/Sun & *The Planets,* episode: *Sun;* original television broadcast, 10/23/1999.

Notes

1.
Sunrise poems #2, *Pasodoblé, and #18, Undercover Reveille,* are without dates; not by error of omission but because I did not record and cannot recall the dates I wrote them. Their position is accurate as to when they were written in relation to the other poems.

2.
"Fun Sun Stuff" was going to be called "Fun Sun Facts" but as science advances, quite often the 'facts' change. Also, some of the Fun Sun Stuff is not fact but merely the dominant existing theory about the sun and related phenomena.

3.
I have less than basic knowledge of science but am nonetheless amazed by the workings of the sun. Being science-challenged did not afford me a springboard of basic tenets from which to write science-fiction-oriented sunrise poem #23, so I titled it "Fiction Science." A cursory interest in the science of the sun ironically led me in a direction away from fact to a scenario of an Earth of different origin; dependent on a different energy source than the sun. It would be nice if out of my ignorance, there is any bliss to be had in "Fiction Science."

4.
Not the science of the sun but thoughts and emotions prompted by witnessing its risings inspired the verse of this book. I hope my recorded experiences of sunrise will in some way fulfill that part of poetry's potential to occasionally light a spark.

Acknowledgments

Very special thanks to my mentor, Harry Ellison.

Special thanks to Barbara Hantman, Juanita Torrence-Thompson, and Joan Reese.

Thank you, Anthony Moscini, Sarah Bedell, Su Polo, Evie Ivy, Anthony Vigorito, Angelo Verga, Robin Hirsch, Joshua Meander, Patricia Carragon, Robin Small-McCarthy, Alan Baxter, Gordon Gilbert, Lorraine Gibney, Bernard Block, Carolyn Reus, Anne Rudder, Daniel Fernandez and Bob McNeil for continuously providing a forum for poetry via performance venues, workshops, 'open mics,' and spaces such as provided by the New York Public Library System staff, to whom I am very grateful. **Thanks**, friends of poetry Norma Levy and Gerhard Maier.

Workshops work for me....
To ***ALL*** members of the workshops I have attended (Harry Ellison's Poets Circle, Riverside Poets Workshop, Jefferson Market Workshop, and Auction House), your creative and constructive input has been instrumental in my development as a poet and also as a person.
Thanks, workshoppers!
Your list, thankfully, is very long. Some of you are: Elliot Abosh, Mark Aiello, Matthew Anish, Lynne Artino, Rose Bernal, Peter Blaxill, Diane Block, Evie Borthwick, Mitchell Cohen, Noel David Cohen, Jessica Cording, Roberta Curley, Robert Dickerson, Charles Dydzuhn, Kathryn Fazio, Linda Fung, Lily Georgick, Robert Gibbons, Nora Glikman, Barbara Gordon, Patrick Hammer Jr., Elyse Hassenbein, Juliet Headrick, Evelyn Huang, Matthew Hupert, Natalia Kerkela, Florence Kindel, Natalie Lardner, Jean Lehrman, Bambi Levine, Barbara Evangeline Litke, Ashley Mabbitt, Marianne McNamara, Duncan Mooney,

Marie Moser, Peggy Murphy, Barbara Newsome, Mary Orovan, Brent Pallas, Stan Raffes, Emma Rose, Anita Rosenblithe, Nicholas Samuels, Shaniki Smith, Miriam Stanley, Catherine Stone, Ian Wold, Elayna Woods and Saul Zachary. May Arnold Agree and Barbara Spector Karr rest in peace.

Big big thanks
to Toni Zimmer for her invaluable word processing expertise, offered with patience and clarity to one who is *so* computer-challenged.

I owe a tremendous debt of gratitude
to Max Zimmer for his encouragement and enthusiasm throughout this project and a special note of thanks for his dedication and quality work on the design and layout of this book.

Thank you ever so much,
Elesia Simpson, for your enduring patience and understanding during the writing process that kept me behind my closed door day after day for hours and hours.

About the Poet

Fred Simpson is proud to be a native and lifelong resident of New York City. Experiencing its diversity and vibrancy has significantly influenced his eclectic taste and style in poetry *and* music. He is a songwriter and accomplished percussionist known to accompany his poetry readings and those of others with his drumming. Fred has been a featured reader at various poetry series including the long-running Saturn Series and Nomad's Choir, both of Manhattan, and the Green Pavilion and Ken Siegelman's Poetry Outreach, both of Brooklyn. His poems appear in a variety of publications such as *Mobius, the Poetry Magazine's 29th & 30th Editions, The Venetian Hour / Dinner with the Muse Vol. II, Estrellas en el Fuego 2014 Anthology, Riverside Poetry Anthology Volumes 13 and 14*, and *The Culvert Chronicles*, an online publication. Fred is currently working on his second book, a series of poems about New York City.

Contact Fred at fredlyric@msn.com

Just Another Sunrise is available in paperback
and ebook, in bookstores and on line.

Signed and inscribed copies of the paperback
are also available from the poet.

I hope I made you look.